Irmgard Kneissler

Super Simple Origami

Irmgard Kneissler

Super
Simple
Origami

Sterling Publishing Co., Inc.
New York

Photos by Alfons Glocker, Aalen/Peter Ruprecht, Dinkelsbühl
Translated by Inger Lasting

Library of Congress Cataloging-in-Publication Data
Kneissler, Irmgard.
    [Kreatives origami. English]
    Super simple origami / Irmgard Kneissler, [translated by
Inger Lasting].
       p.   cm.
    ISBN 0-8069-6471-5
    1. Origami. I. Title.
TT870.K57213   1999
736'.982—DC21   99-35625
                               CIP

20 19 18 17 16 15 14

Published in 2006 by Sterling Publishing Company, Inc.
387 Park Avenue South, New York, N.Y. 10016
Originally published in Germany by Ravensburger Buchverlag
under the title *Kreatives Origami*
© 1996 by Ravensburger Buchverlag
English translation © 1999 by Sterling Publishing Co., Inc.
Distributed in Canada by Sterling Publishing
c/o Canadian Manda Group, 165 Dufferin Street
Toronto, Ontario, Canada M6K 3H6
Distributed in the United Kingdom by GMC Distribution Services
Castle Place, 166 High Street, Lewes, East Sussex, England BN7 1XU
Distributed in Australia by Capricorn Link (Australia) Pty. Ltd.
P.O. Box 704, Windsor, NSW 2756, Australia

Sterling ISBN 978-0-8069-6471-3 (hardcover)
          ISBN 978-0-8069-6525-3 (paperback)

For information about custom editions, special sales, premium and
corporate purchases, please contact Sterling Special Sales
Department at 800-805-5489 or specialsales@sterlingpublishing.com.

Contents

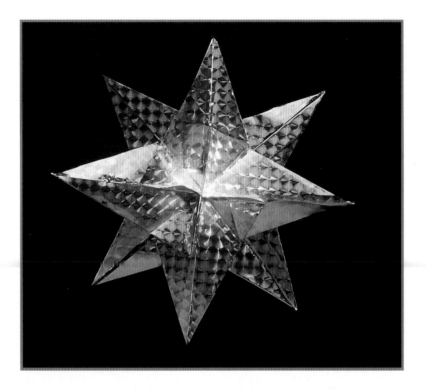

Origami has become so well known in the Western world today that it is hard to imagine the art of paper-folding without this tradition-rich Japanese folding technique. It's understandable, because the ancient art of origami offers everyone highly satisfying ways to turn a simple piece of paper into a variety of amazing and surprisingly charming figures and forms. This old Asian handicraft also complements, in an extraordinary way, the present-day desire of many individuals for an understanding of technical connections and logical progressions—without suppressing the folder's individual creativity and fantasy. An essential characteristic of the origami art is the development of the figures from various basic forms. Those presented here represent the possibilities—some of the many figures that can be created. Just simply recreating these forms and figures provides, in itself, rich experience. The skills gained in the process make it possible to create other new and perhaps entirely original figures, bound only by one's own imagination.

Irmgard Kneissler

not normally available for purchase. Each origami figure is an original, thus something special. The hand-folded figures are suitable for use on place cards or invitations and as special decorations, and because they are unusual and unique, they receive much attention and appreciation. Many forms make charming and original table decorations, especially since some can be folded from paper napkins.

Material

Actually, paper is all that is needed to do paper folding. The paper used should be as thin as possible, should not rip while folding, and should be stretch-proof. Paper that is stretch-proof will not become misshapen or wavy at the fold creases. For origami, it is good to have paper that is colored on one side and white on the other. It will help in learning to fold, and the second color will add a creative element to the work.

You may need a good pair of scissors for cutting the folding sheets if the paper is not precut to size. A "folding bone," used to burnish creases, may be helpful, although using a thumbnail works as well. Glue is not needed in order to make the forms themselves, but to attach them to card backing or onto a letter, or to decorate a gift; or if you want to decorate the figures, such as gluing eyes onto an animal form (a practice not, however, in keeping with strict Japanese tradition).

What can you do with origami?

Origami figures are not "manufactured" and so are

Basic rules of the folding art

1. Always work on a solid, flat surface.

2. Make all folds as precise and straight as possible.

3. Crease all folds thoroughly, with a "folding bone" or thumbnail.

4. Select a paper that is suitable in color and quality to the figure you wish to make.

5. After each step of the fold, position the model exactly as shown in the drawing.

6. During each step of the fold, refer to and keep in mind the next work sketch, as it shows the results of the fold you are making.

Symbols and Terminology

Before we start the instructions for working the forms, here are explanations of the symbols that occur over and over in this book, and of important folding terms that are used.

Here, letters serve as symbols in the drawings to identify the various parts of a form. Symbols for points or other parts of a figure that are "below" or "inside" appear in a circle (1).

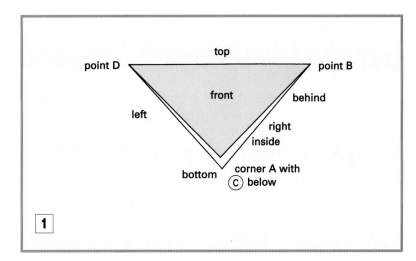

"up"= right angle to figure body
"top"= side away from figure body
"bottom"= side toward figure body
(2)

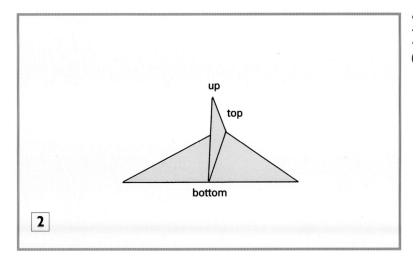

dashed line = valley fold
dotted line = mountain fold
plain line = a fold
dashed-dotted line = crease (3)

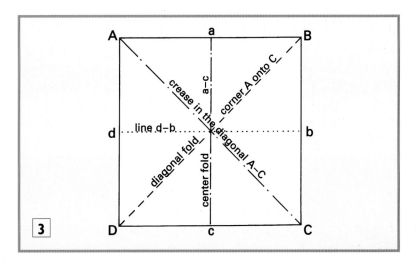

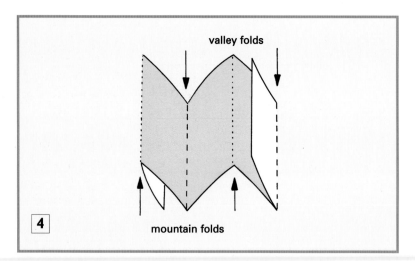

"Valley folds" fold forward, toward the folder; "mountain folds" fold toward the back, away from the folder (**4**).

A "reverse fold to the outside" is represented by a dashed line; a "reverse fold to the inside" is represented by a dotted line (**5**).

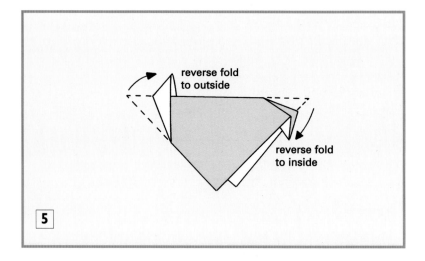

Forms frequently occurring in folding (**6**).

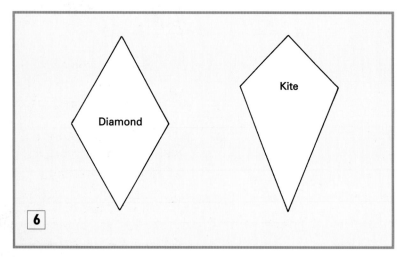

ORIGAMI TERMS AT A GLANCE

Below: edge, corner, or point pointing towards the folder (see **1**, page 9).

Center fold: runs through the center of the folding job, or through the part in the process of being folded (see **3**, page 9).

Corner: can be rectangular or an obtuse angle (see **1**, page 9).

Crease: to fold and unfold again as the line indicates; a fold unfolded (see **3**, page 9).

Diagonal: a line running diagonally through the center from corner to corner (see **3**, page 9).

Fold over: fold a part of the folding job over into an existing crease on the other side.

Front: visible side turned toward the viewer (see **1**, page 9).

Inside: everything that is between the back and front sides. The symbols for the parts, corners, or points that lie on the inside are encircled in the diagrams (see **1**, page 9).

Line: a connection from one point to another, for instance, line **d–b** (see **3**, page 9).

Mountain fold: a fold that is carried out away from the folder. The inside fold crease points upward, forming a mountain (see **4**, page 10).

On top: edge, corner, or point pointing away from the folder (see **1**, page 9).

Outside: back and front sides of the fold (see **1**, page 9).

Point: an acute angle (see **1**, page 9).

Pull: grasp the point indicated and pull it onto the point marked.

Reverse fold: reverse the existing fold, exactly in its crease, to the opposite side.

Reverse fold to the outside: the sides once lying on the inside now lie in the back and front on the outside of the folding paper (see **5**, page 10).

Reverse fold to the inside: the sides once on the outside, after completing the step now lie on the inside between the front and back parts of the folding job (see **5**, page 10).

Right, left: parts to the right or left of the center crease (see **1**, page 9).

Turn: rotate the entire form around the center point, without lifting the folding paper.

Turn around: turn the front side on the base over to the back, so the back side is now in front.

Unfold: reverse the last folding step.

Up: vertically standing on the flat fold (see **2**, page 9).

Valley fold: a fold carried out toward the person doing the fold. The inside fold crease extends downward, forming a valley (see **4**, page 10).

Basic Form A

Square sheet of folding paper, colored side back. Crease diagonal **A–C;** valley fold the dashed lines at corners **B** and **D** (1).

Finished basic form A (2).

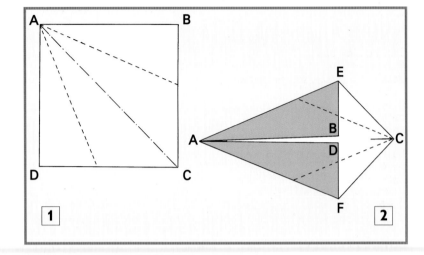

Basic Form B

Square sheet of folding paper, colored side back. Valley folds in diagonals, unfold.

Mountain folds in the center creases, unfold.

Pull points **b** and **d** onto point **a** so that point **c** also falls onto point **a** (1).

Finished basic form B (2).

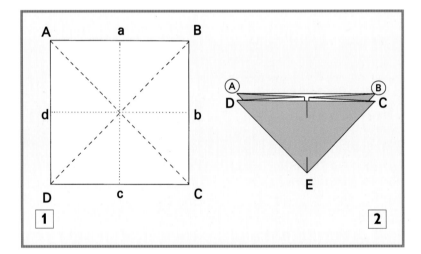

Basic Form C

Square folding paper, colored side back. Crease center folds.

With valley folds, bring all four corners to the center fold (1).

Finished basic form C (2).

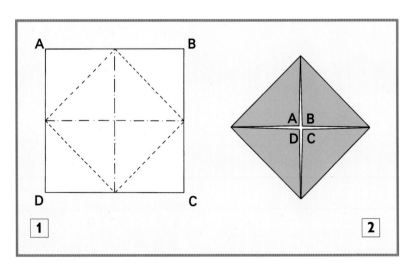

Basic Form D

Square sheet of folding paper, colored side back.

Mountain folds in the diagonals, unfold.

Valley folds in center creases, unfold.

Pull corners **B** and **D** onto corner **A**, so corner **C** also falls onto corner **A** (**1**).

The finished basic form D (**2**).

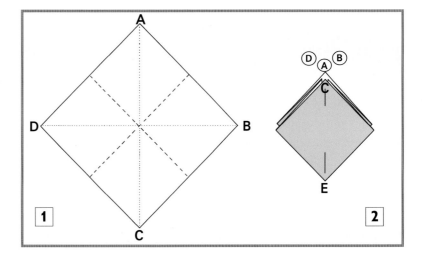

Basic Form E

Starting point: basic form D

In the dashed-dotted lines 1, crease the corners **F** and **G** to the center fold.

In the dashed-dotted line 2, fold corner **E** over it (**1**).

Bring up corner **C** in crease 2 just formed. At the same time, press corners **G** and **F** to the center crease (**2**).

Turn over to the back; repeat steps shown in illustrations **1** and **2**. Turn over (**3**).

The finished basic form E (**4**).

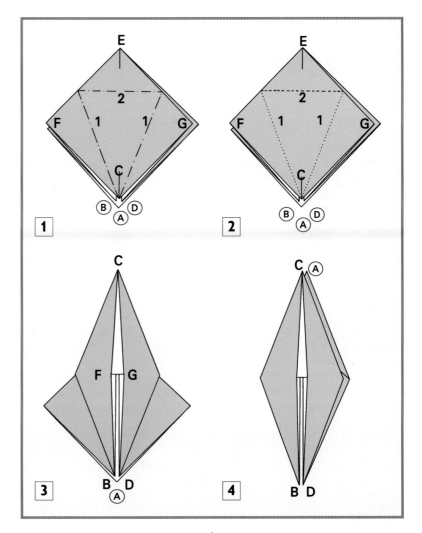

The duck figure can be individualized by simple changes of the reverse folds.

The body can be made shorter, the neck longer; the duck can look up, or down.

Starting point: basic form A

Valley folds in dashed lines (**1**).

Valley fold in center crease (**2**).

Reverse folds outside in the dashed lines at A and C (**3**).

Reverse fold outside in the dashed line at point **A**. Reverse fold inside in the dotted line at point **C**. Mountain folds front and back at corners **G** and **H** (**4**).

Reverse folds inside and outside at point **A** to form the beak (**5**).

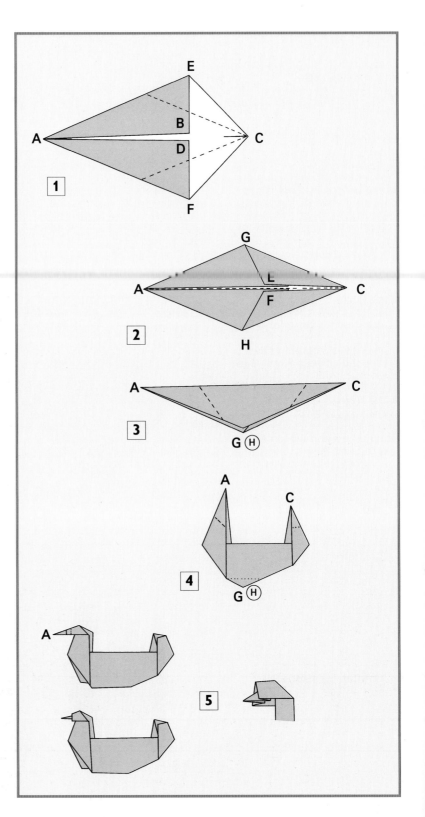

Fish (as wind sock)

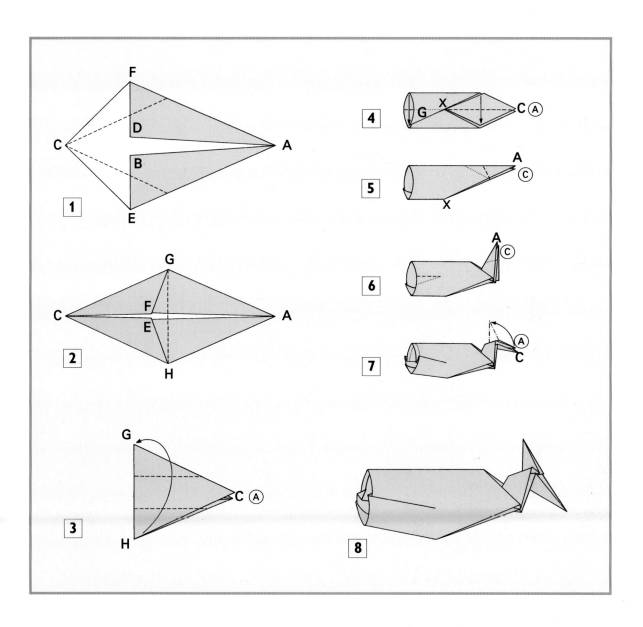

Made in miniature, this fish (mounted on a drinking straw) can decorate a tall summertime drink or party-atmosphere refreshment.

Starting point: basic form A

A size of folding paper at least 19.5 inches (50 cm) square.

At corner **C**, valley folds in the dashed lines (**1**).

Valley fold in the dashed line, point **C** on point **A** (**2**).

Valley fold in the dashed lines, then tuck corner **H** into corner **G** (**3**).

Form a tube from the figure obtained, and turn it into position as shown in illustration **5** (**4**).

Reverse folds inside and outside at point **A/C** (fold together) (**5**).

Reverse fold inside at point **A/C**. Form the mouth at the round opening by mountain and valley folds in the front and back (**6**).

Fold point **A** upward to the fin. Fasten the mouth creases by tucking in the inside corners (**7**).

The finished model (**8**).

Every little monkey can have a different look, by a simple adjustment of the reverse folds.

Starting point: basic form A

At point **C**, valley folds in the dashed lines (**1**).

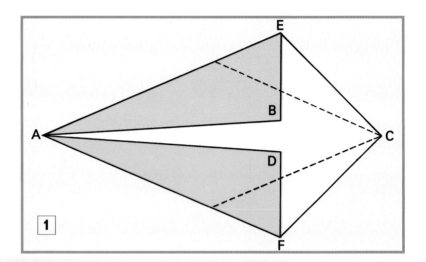

At point **C**, valley fold left in the dashed line (**2**).

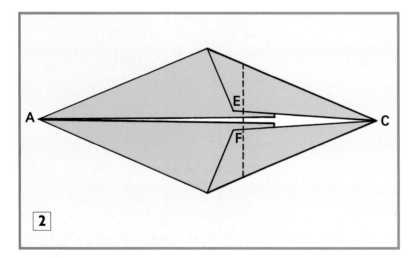

At point **C**, valley fold to the right in the dashed line (**3**).

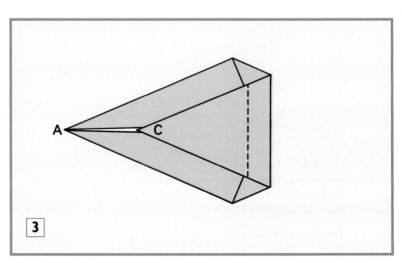

At point **C**, move the points **X** into the position shown in illustration **6** by means of valley folds in the dashed lines and mountain folds in the dotted lines (**4**).

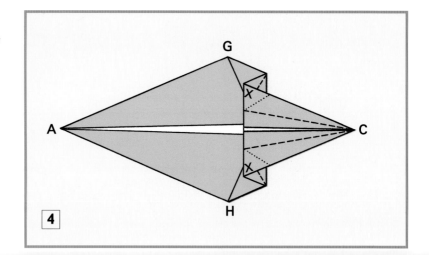

Valley fold in the center crease (**5**).

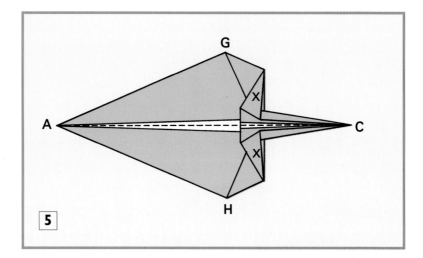

Valley fold in the dashed line— only the front sheet of paper. Simultaneously, pull point **A** into the position shown in illustration **8**. Crease the mountain fold that is forming in the dotted line (**6**).

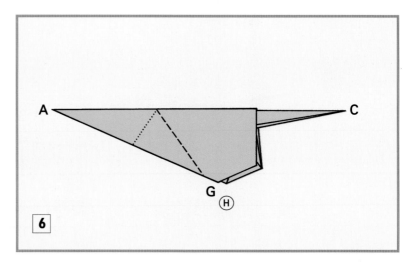

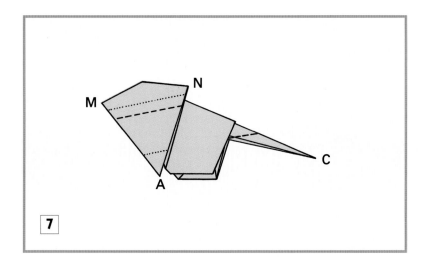

7

Form the head by means of mountain and valley folds at point **A**. At point **C**, reverse fold to the outside (**7**).

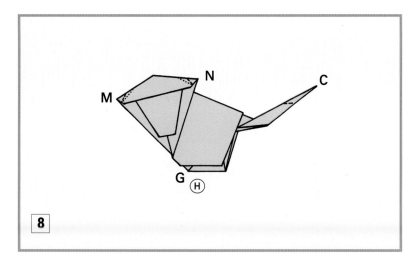

8

Form the ears at corners **M** and **N** by reverse folds inside and outside. At point **C**, reverse fold outside (**8**).

The finished model, enlarged (**9**).

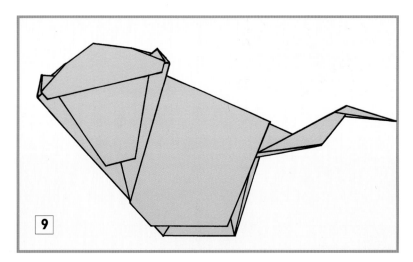

9

Rose

This pretty rose, folded from individual layers of a paper napkin, makes a unique and appropriate table decoration.

Starting point: basic form C

Once more, fold all corners to the center point (**1**).

For a third time, fold all corners to the center point (**2**).

Turn over (**3**), and again fold all corners to the center point (**4**).

Carefully pull forward, across corners **E**, **F**, **G**, and **H**, the corners lying on top in the center point, until they poke up (**5**).

Simultaneously, lightly press corners **E**, **F**, **G**, and **H** toward the outside; see enlarged partial illustration (**6**).

After completing the work on the first four corners, also pull forward the four other corners in the back (**7**).

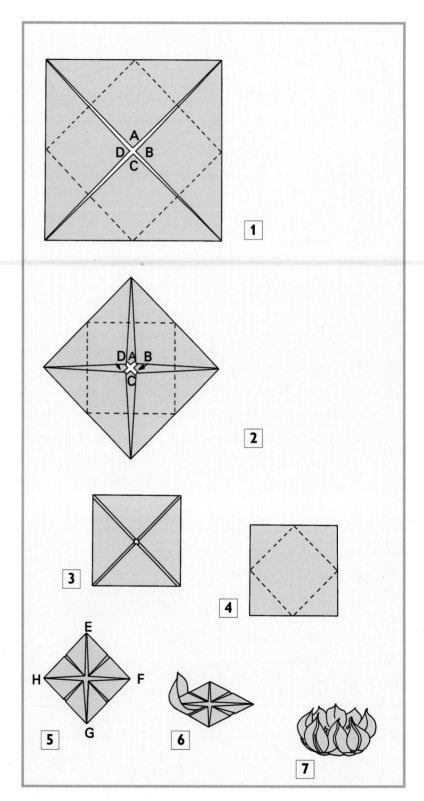

Penguins, fancy-dressed in their tuxedoes, and a few chunks of white plastic foam, for ice, can turn the table at a children's party into an arctic landscape.

Starting point: basic form A

Valley folds in the dashed lines (**1**).

Fold point **A** to point **C**, unfold. In the crease just created, fold points **B** and **D**, lying inside on the right, outward to the left (**2**).

Valley folds at points **B** and **D** (**3**).

Mountain fold in the center crease (**4**).

Turn model. Pull point **B** to the right (see next illustration). Turn model, and repeat with point **D**, turn (**5**).

At point **A**, reverse fold inside (**6**).

Reverse fold inside at points **A** and **C** (**7**).

Form the beak by reverse folds inside and outside at point **A**. Valley folds at points **B** and **D**. Reverse fold inside at point **C** (**8**).

The finished model (**9**).

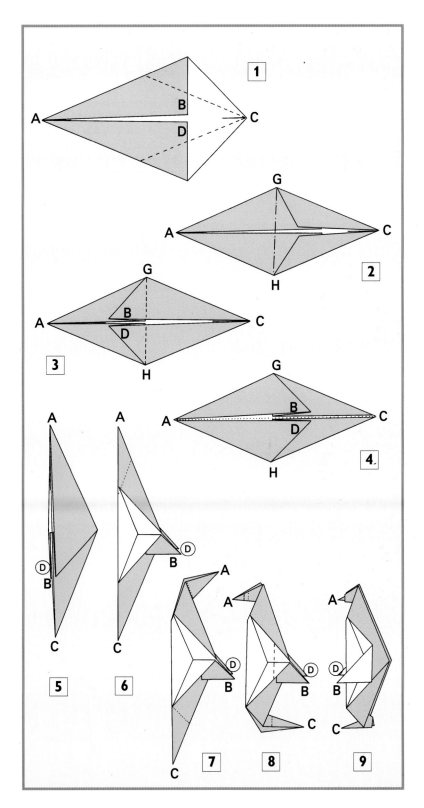

This feline figure requires two folding parts. The folded paper to make the head is about half the size as the folding paper used for the body.

HEAD

Starting point: basic form A

Valley folds at corners **C**, **B**, and **D** (**1**).

Valley folds in lines 1 at corners **B** and **D**, and in line 2 at corner **C** (**2**).

Valley fold at point **A**. Tuck point **A** under point **C**. Mountain folds at points **E** and **F** in the dotted lines, and valley folds in the dashed lines (**3**).

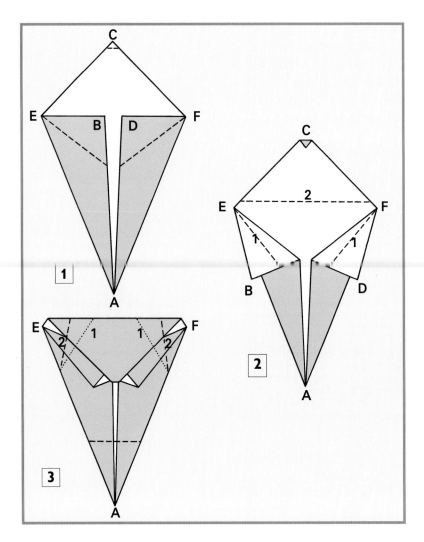

Mountain fold in the dotted line on top. Mountain and valley fold in lines **1** and **2** (**4**).

Finished head (**5**).

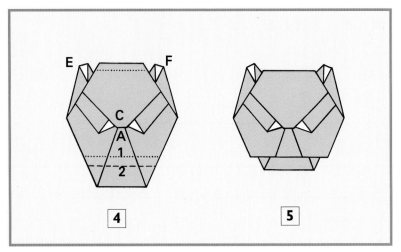

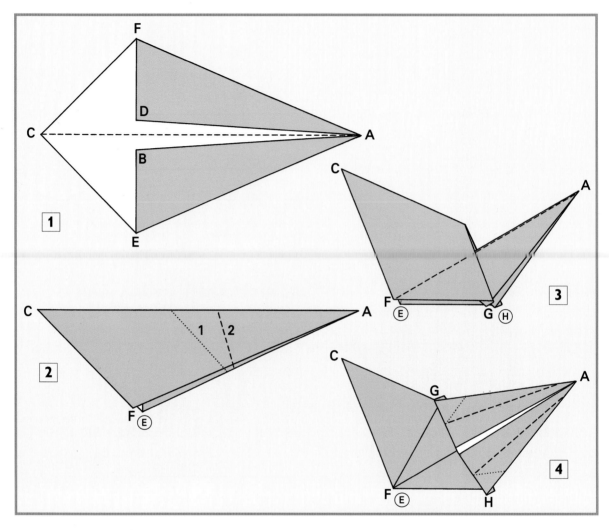

BODY

Starting point: basic form A

Valley fold in center crease (**1**).

At point **A**, reverse folds inward and outward (**2**).

Bring corner **G** upward by valley fold in the dashed line **A – F** (**3**).

Valley folds at point **A**. By mountain folds in the dotted lines, **G** and **H** will fall on the points shown in illustration **5** (**4**).

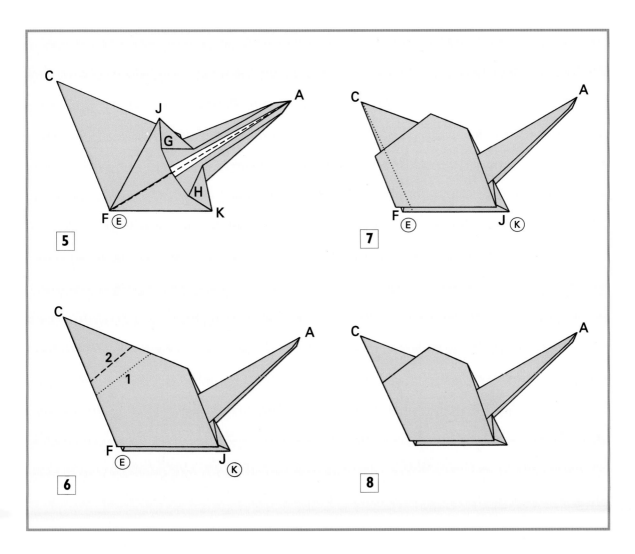

Valley fold in the tail's center crease, **J** onto **K** (**5**).

At point **C**, reverse folds inward and outward (**6**).

At point **C**, mountain folds in front and behind (**7**).

Finished body model (**8**).

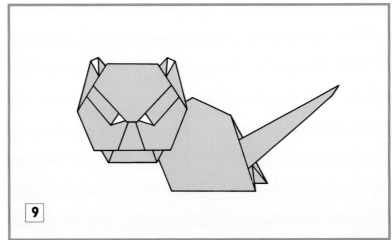

Hang or glue the head to point **C** of the body (**9**).

The finished blossoms are not just beautiful-to-look-at flowers, but can also serve as especially pretty folds for small letters and notes.

FLOWER I

Starting point: basic form A

At corner **C**, valley folds in the dashed lines (**1**).

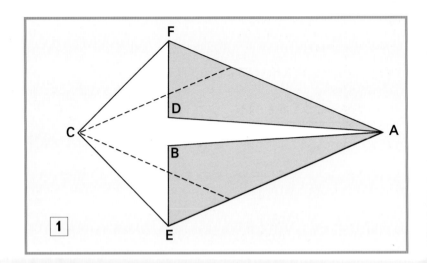

Valley fold in the dashed lines, outward to the right, the inside corners **B** and **D** (**2**).

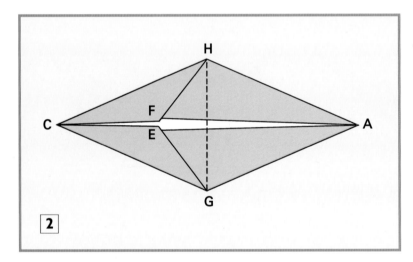

Turn the model over (**3**).

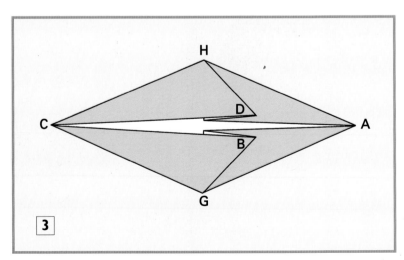

At point **D**, fashion the form of a kite by the indicated mountain and valley folds (**4**).

Valley fold at point **D**. Fold point **B** like **D** (**5**).

At points **A** and **C**, valley folds in the dashed lines (**6**).

By mountain and valley folds, bring points **A** and **C** into position shown in illustration **8** (**7**).

By mountain and valley folds in the lines indicated, bring points **A** and **C** flat onto the model's center (**8**).

Mountain fold in the dotted line at point **A**. Repeat at point **C**. Tuck points **A** and **C** under points **B** and **D** (**9**).

The finished blossom (**10**).

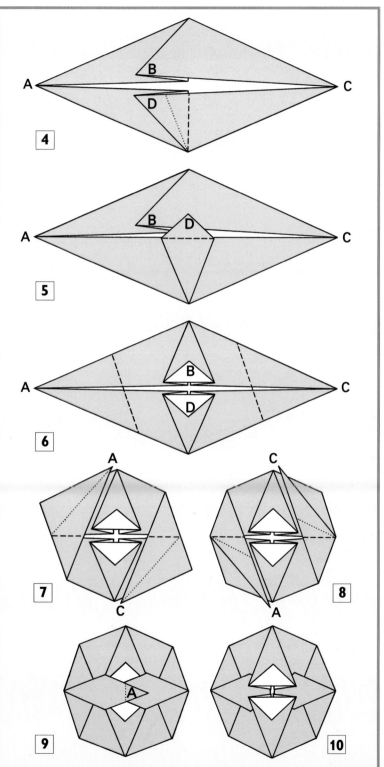

FLOWER II

Starting point: basic form A

Fold the basic form from all four corners of the folding paper and unfold again. Fold edge **A – B** in the existing crease to the center crease, then fold edge **A – D** in the existing crease to the center crease (**1**).

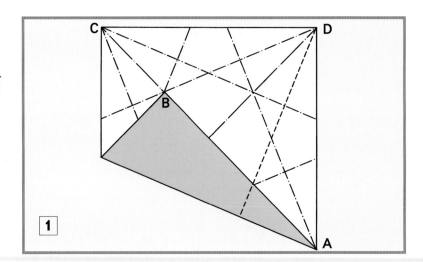

By a valley fold in the dashed line and a mountain fold in the dotted line, **X** falls onto the point shown in illustration **3** (**2**).

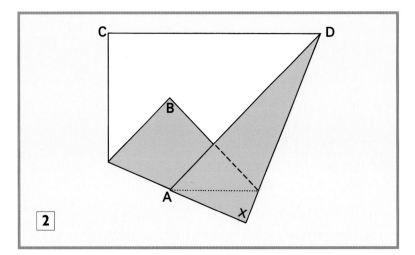

Fold in the existing crease edge **C – D** to the center crease (**3**).

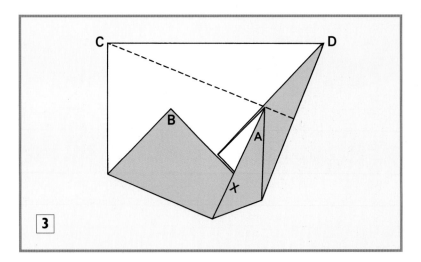

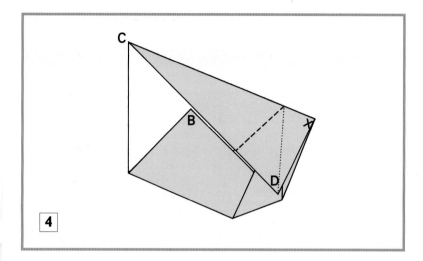

4

By a valley fold in the dashed line and a mountain fold in the dotted line, **X** falls onto the point shown in illustration **5** (**4**).

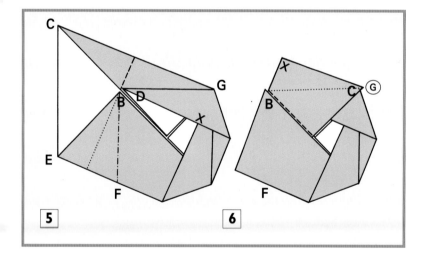

5   **6**

Fold edge **B – E** in the dotted line inwards under crease **B – F**. Simultaneously, fold point **C** onto corner **G** (**5**).

By means of a valley fold in the dashed line and a mountain fold in the dotted line, **X** falls onto the point shown in illustration **7** (**6**).

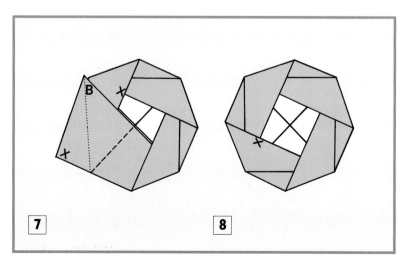

7   **8**

By means of a valley fold in the dashed line and a mountain fold in the dotted line, **X** falls onto the point shown in illustration **8**. Tuck point **B** under point **A** (**7**).

The finished blossom (**8**).

STEM WITH LEAF

Starting point: basic form A

At point **A**, valley folds in the dashed lines (**1**).

At point **C**, valley folds in the dashed lines (**2**).

Fold point **C** onto the model by a valley fold in the dashed line (**3**).

Mountain fold in the center crease (**4**).

Pull point **C** the leaf—lightly sideways, and crease again the changed lower creases (**5**).

Glue flower I or flower II to the stem (**6**).

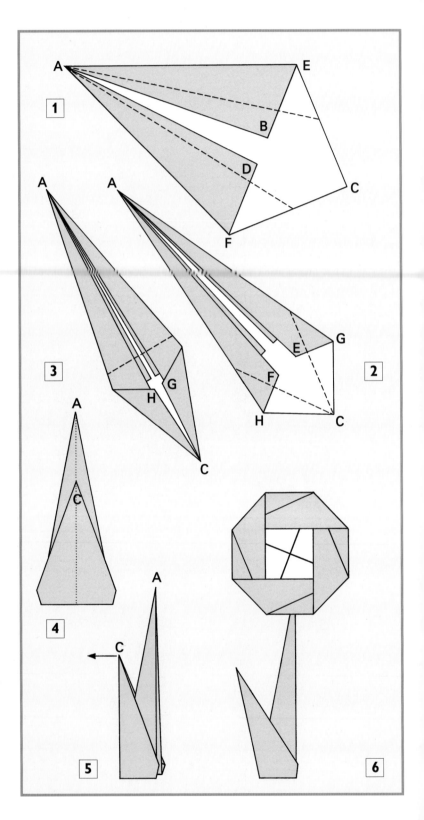

If best wishes enter a home in the form of butterflies, they get special attention. A cheery note or greeting can be written on the white side of the sheet of paper before folding.

Starting point: basic form B

Valley folds in the dashed lines at points **C** and **D** (**1**).

Turn over (**2**).

Valley fold in the dashed line to bring up points **E**, **C**, and **D** (**3**).

Fold points **C** and **D** down, at the same time pressing points **X** towards the center (**4**).

Mountain and valley folds at point **E**. Valley fold in the center crease (**5**).

Valley folds in the dashed line in front and behind…(**6**)

…and the butterfly unfolds (**7**).

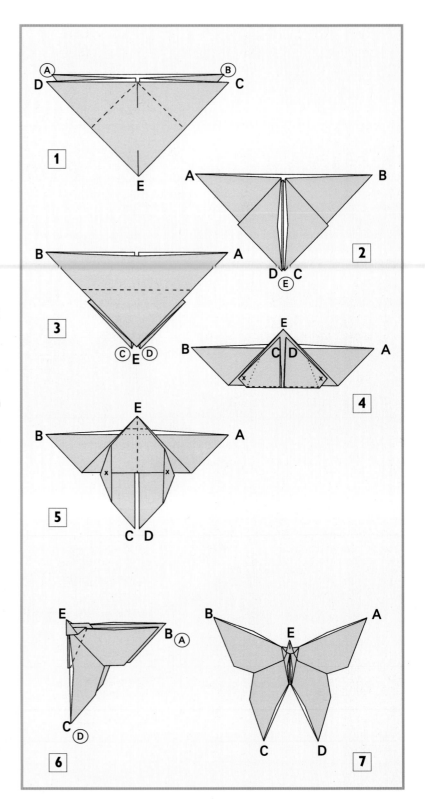

Cormorants fashioned from larger-size (15 inch/40 cm square) folding sheets will lend a special touch to a festive fish-dinner table.

Starting point: basic form A

By valley folds in the dashed lines, bring the edges **A – E** and **A – F** to the center crease (**1**).

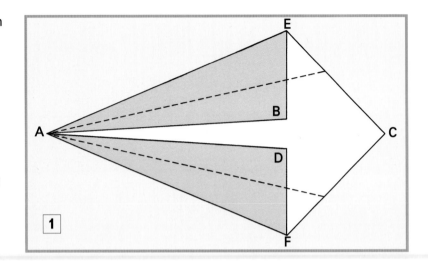

Valley fold in the center crease (**2**).

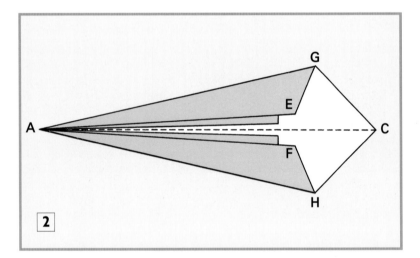

At point **A**, reverse fold inside in the dotted line (**3**).

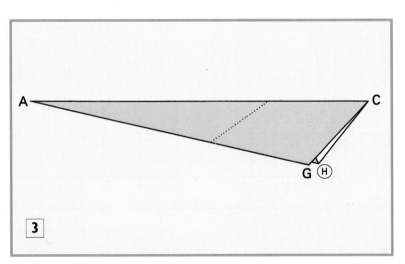

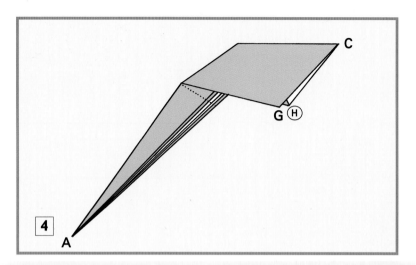

At point **A**, reverse fold toward the inside in the dotted line (**4**).

At point **A**, reverse fold in the dotted line toward the inside. By reverse fold to the inside, bring corner **X** into the inner part of the fold (**5**).

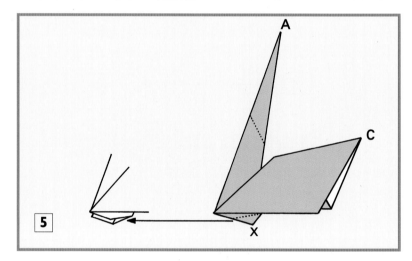

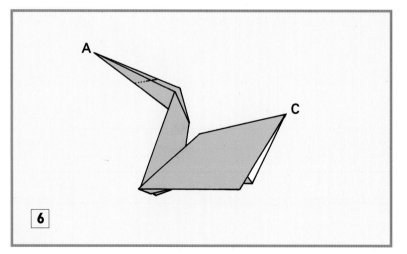

At point **A**, reverse fold toward the outside along the indicated line (**6**).

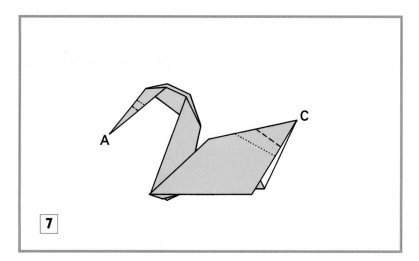

At point **A**, fashion the beak by reverse folds to the inside and outside. At point **C**, fashion the tail by reverse folds to the inside and the outside (**7**).

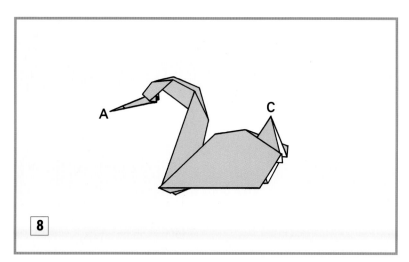

At point **A**, bend the beak down (**8**).

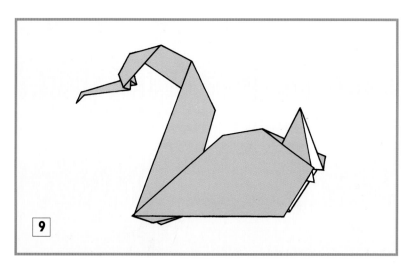

The finished model, enlarged (**9**).

Here is one very beautiful table decoration that every guest will want to take home, so you'll have to make several. The tulips will stand fast and securely, if you place a coin in the stalk.

Starting point: basic form E

Rotate the basic form. Fold upward point **C** in front, and point **A** in the back (**1**).

Valley folds right and left, in front and back, in the dashed lines. Valley fold at corner **E**, in the dashed-dotted line, and unfold again (**2**).

Press the tulip blossom open, from the center outward, and flatten out corner **E** (**3**).

Fold a stem with leaf as given on page 34, and glue the tulip onto it. The finished tulip (**4**).

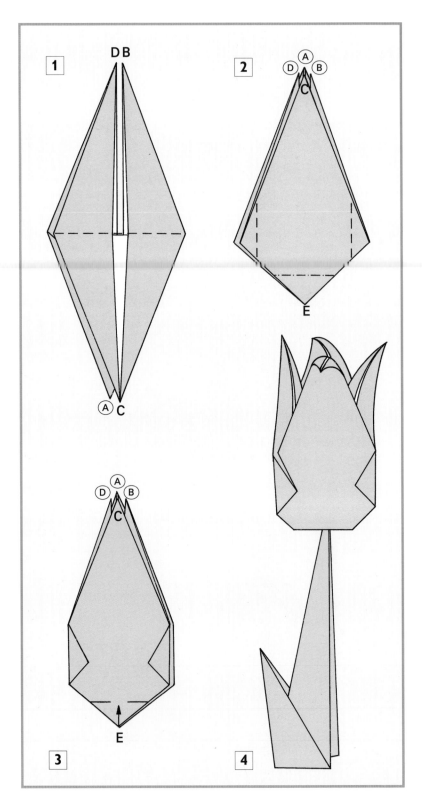

In working this model, make sure that the folding sheet used for the owl is only ¼ the length of the side of the folding sheet for the tree.

OWL

Starting point: basic form A

Fold point **A**, before folding the basic form, onto the folding sheet, so that it lies inside, as shown in the illustration. Valley folds in the dashed lines at corners **B** and **D** (**1**).

At corner **C**, valley fold in the dashed line (**2**).

By mountain and valley folds, form the beak at corner **C**, and the ears at corners **E** and **F** (**3**).

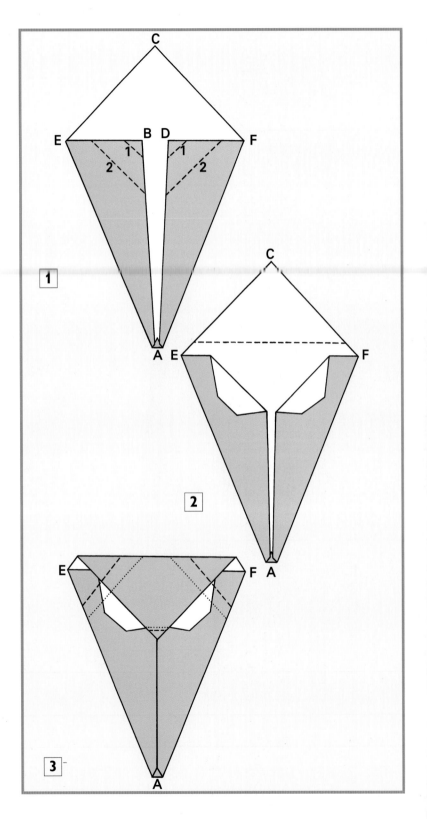

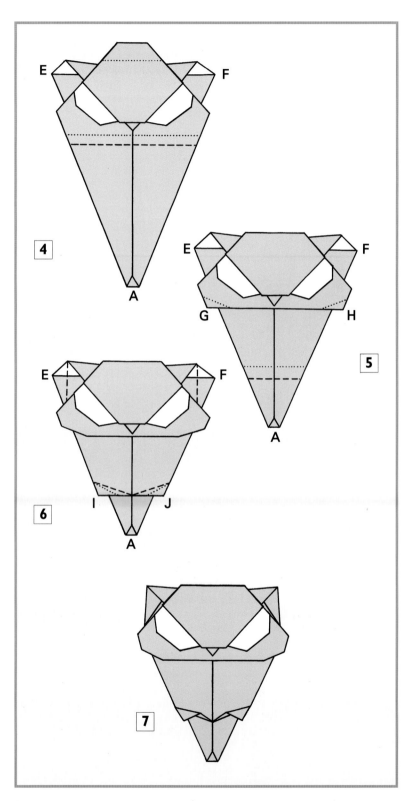

Mountain fold in the dotted line on top. Form the head by mountain and valley folds below the beak (**4**).

Mountain folds at corners **G** and **H**.

Fashion the tail at point **A** by mountain and valley folds (**5**).

At corners **I** and **J**, form the feet by mountain and valley folds. At corners **E** and **F**, tuck the outer edges into the inner sides of the ears (**6**).

The finished owl (**7**).

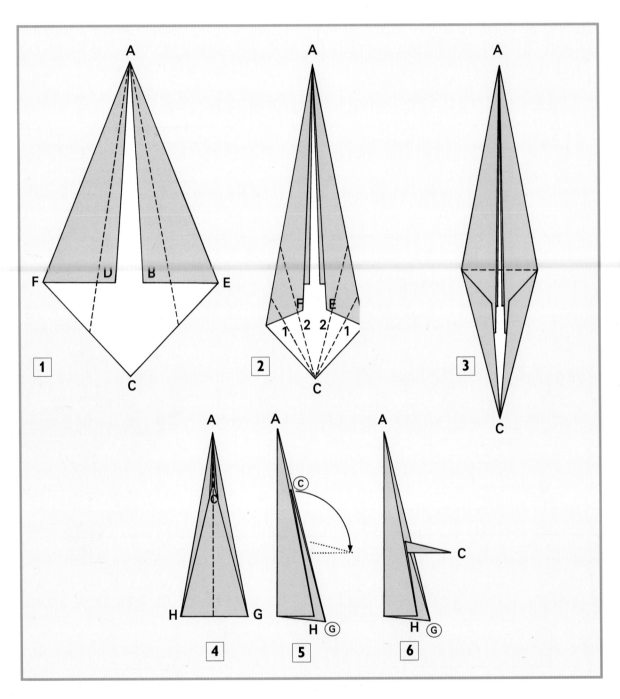

TREE

Starting point: basic form A

At point **A**, valley folds in the dashed lines (**1**).

At point **C**, valley folds in the dashed lines 1 and 2 (**2**).

Fold point **C** in the dashed line onto folding figure (**3**).

Valley fold in the center crease (**4**).

By reverse fold to the inside, fold the inside-lying point **C** sideways, outward (**5**).

The finished model (**6**).

This star shape makes a fine personal touch to correspondences, with its back point tucked into a slit cut into the writing paper. To make an eight-point star, you can glue two stars together by their front or back sides. Folding out the point that lies to the back provides an additional element of decoration.

Starting point: basic form E

Reverse folds to the inside at points **B** and **D**. By a valley fold in the dashed line, bring point **C** down, and turn the fold over (**1**).

Valley folds in the dashed lines at corners **B** and **D** (**2**).

The finished model (**3**).

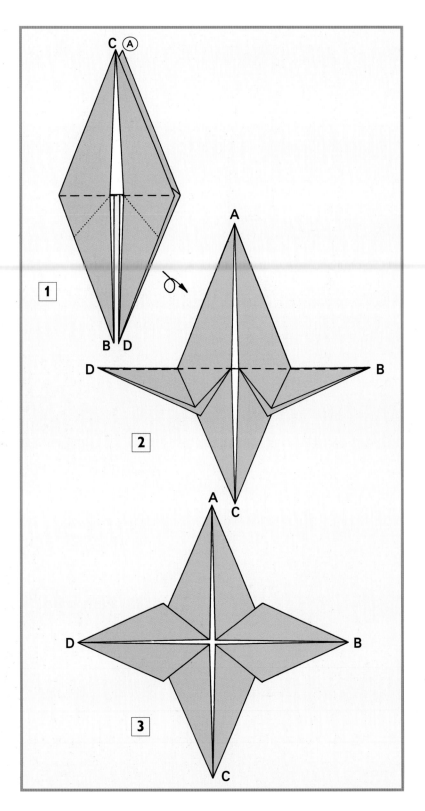

These very simple-to-do folding figures are fun spring holiday projects for children. They also add a nice touch to a bonnet, basket, or table.

Starting point: basic form A

Valley fold in the center crease (**1**).

At point **A**, form the tail by reverse fold outward. At point **C**, fashion the beak by reverse fold to the inside (**2**).

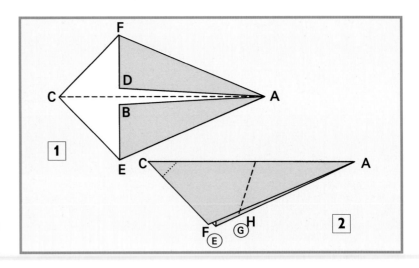

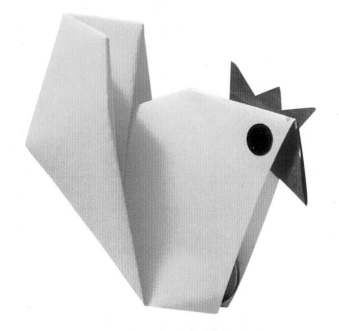

HEN

Reverse fold to the inside at point **A**. The chicken must stand on the edges **E – F** and **F – H**. If necessary, pull point **A** further over toward the head (**3**).

Cut out the hen's red comb and glue it on (**4**).

ROOSTER

Fold the hen (page 50) up to illustration **2**. The folding sheet for the rooster can be somewhat larger than the one for the hen. At point **A**, reverse fold outward (**3**).

At point **A**, reverse fold to the inside (**4**).

Cut out the rooster's red comb and glue it on (**5**).

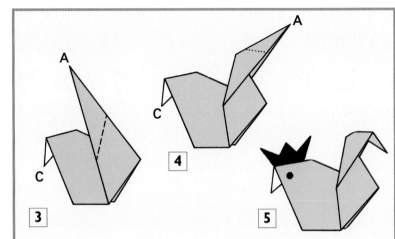

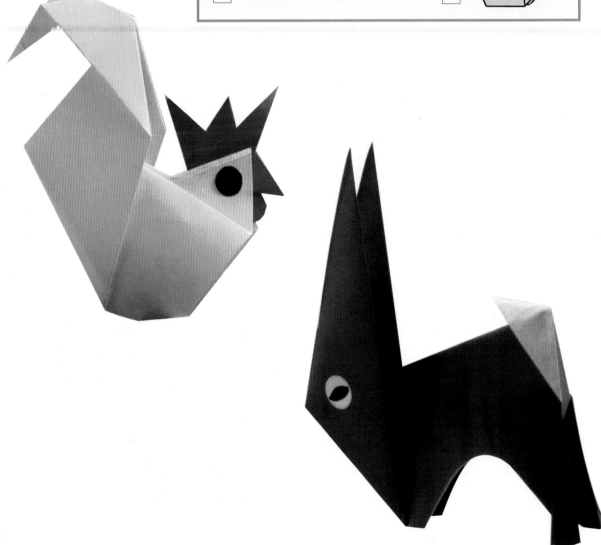

RABBIT

Starting point: basic form A

At corner **C**, valley fold in the dashed line, and mountain fold in the dotted lines.

Corner **C** will now lie on the backside of the folding job (**1**).

Valley fold in the center crease (**2**).

At point **A**, reverse fold outward (**3**).

At point **A**, cut the ears open (**4**), and this very simple figure is finished.

The rabbit, however, can be refined a little bit. For this, cut out the hatched part, front and back (**5**).

Lightly pull out point **C**. Valley folds in the dashed lines, front and back of the hind legs (**6**).

The finished refined model (**7**).

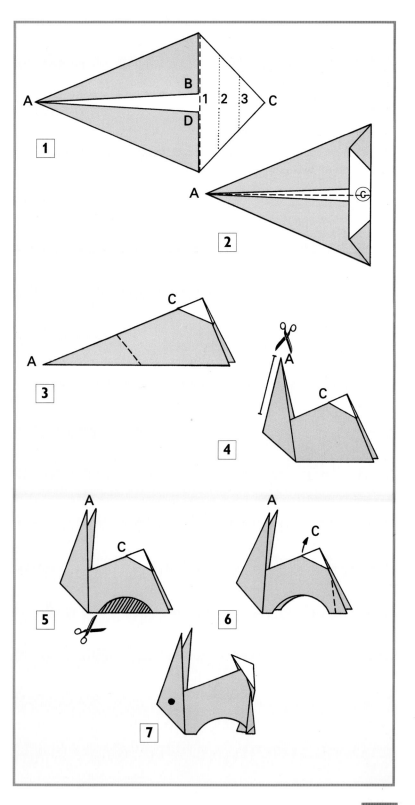

This pinwheel will turn without problems if the center is held together with glue front and back. Left unglued (and without a stick), these folded figures can carry cute invitations to a child's birthday party.

Starting point: basic form C

Fold corners **A** and **C** backward onto the center point.
Fold corners **F** and **H** to the front, and corners **E** and **G** to the back onto the center point (**1**).

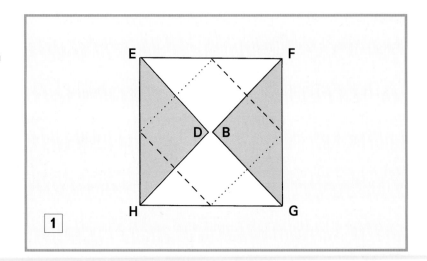

At point **A**, mountain fold in the dotted line, and valley fold in the dashed line (**2**).

At point **A**, valley folds in the dashed lines in the sequence indicated (**3**).

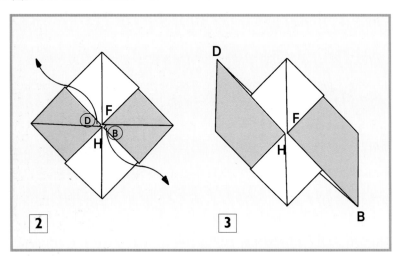

Pull out corners **A** and **C** in the same way (**4**).

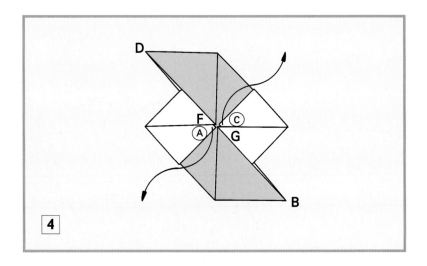

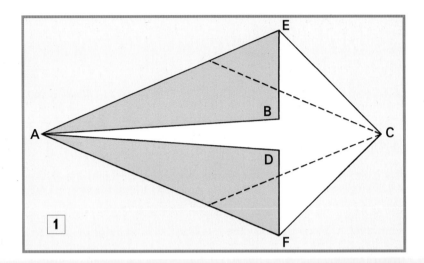lephant

Elephants are a favorite in any form. This one, created from a simple piece of paper, large or small, is very special.

Starting point: basic form A

At point **C**, valley folds in the dashed lines (**1**).

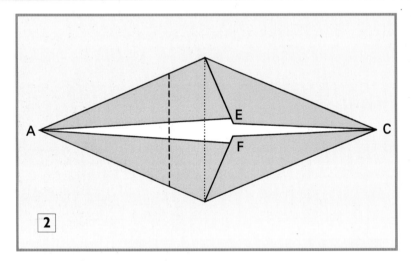

At point **A**, mountain fold in the dotted line, and valley fold in the dashed line (**2**).

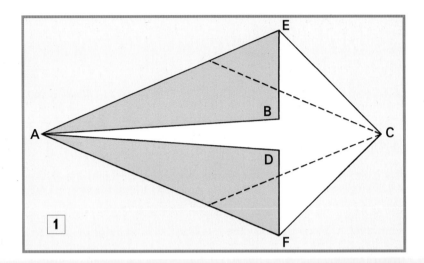

At point **A**, valley folds in the dashed lines in the sequence indicated (**3**).

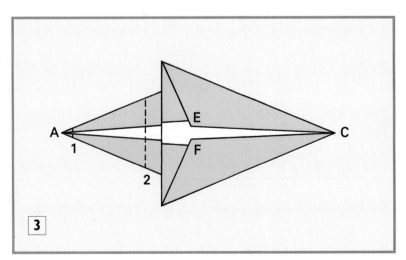

At point **A**, valley fold in the dashed line (**4**).

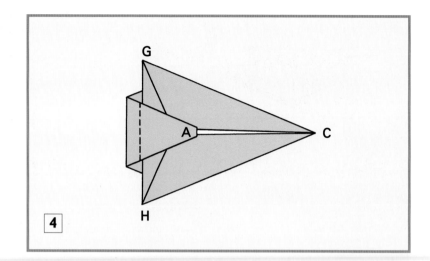

By means of mountain folds, the points **X** will fall into the position shown in illustration **6**, and small triangular cones will form (**5**).

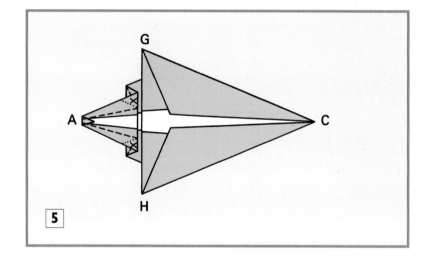

Valley fold in center crease, point **G** onto point **H** (**6**).

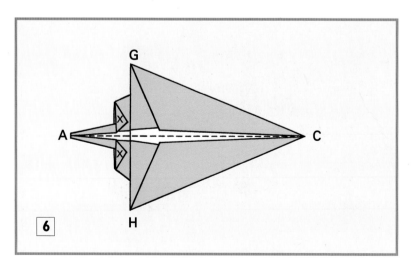

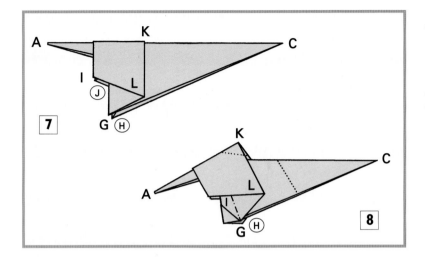

Change the creases **G – H** and **H – J** (front edge of the front feet), as shown in illustration **8**. By doing so, corner **K** automatically moves upward (**7**).

At corner **K**, reverse fold inside. At point **C**, reverse fold inside (**8**).

At corner **C**, reverse fold inside. Point **A**, the trunk, is flexible, and can be moved into any position desired (**9**).

At corner **L**, reverse folds inside, in front and behind, so that the corner will lie under the ear. Form the tail by twisting it (**10**).

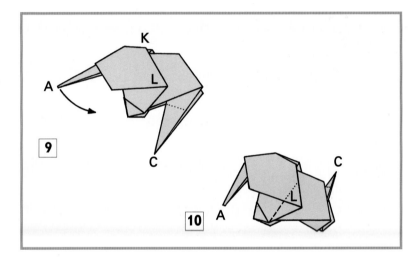

The finished elephant, shown in enlarged form in the photo (**11**).

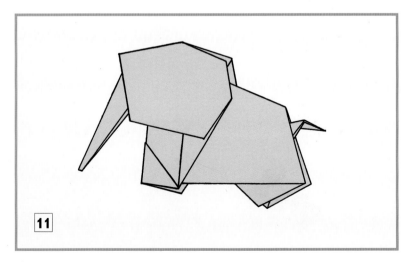

The bodies of the ghostly masked figures prancing mischievously in the photo opposite have been freely created from basic form E.

MASK I

Starting point: basic form A

Valley fold at corner **C**. Valley fold at point **A** (**1**).

At point **A**, valley fold (**2**).

At corner **C**, valley fold (**3**).

At point **A**, valley fold (**4**).

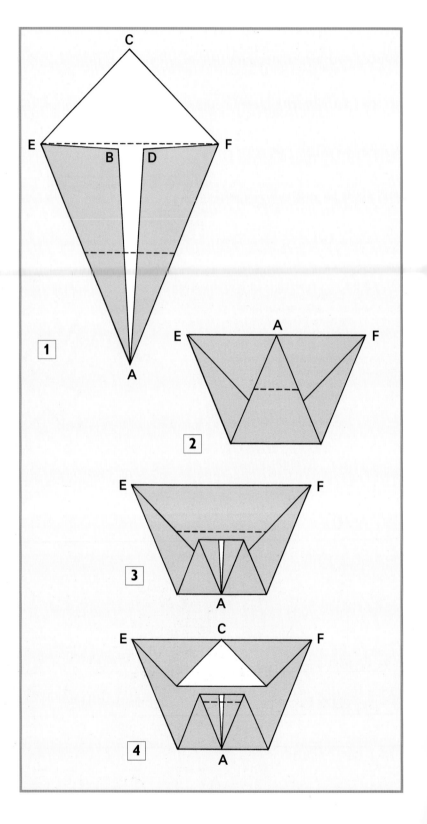

Valley fold at point **A** (**5**).

Valley fold at point **A** (**6**).

At corner **C**, valley folds in the dashed lines **1** and **2**. Tuck corner **C** under the edge of the fold, as shown in illustration **8** (**7**).

Mountain folds at points **E** and **F** (**8**).

The finished mask (**9**).

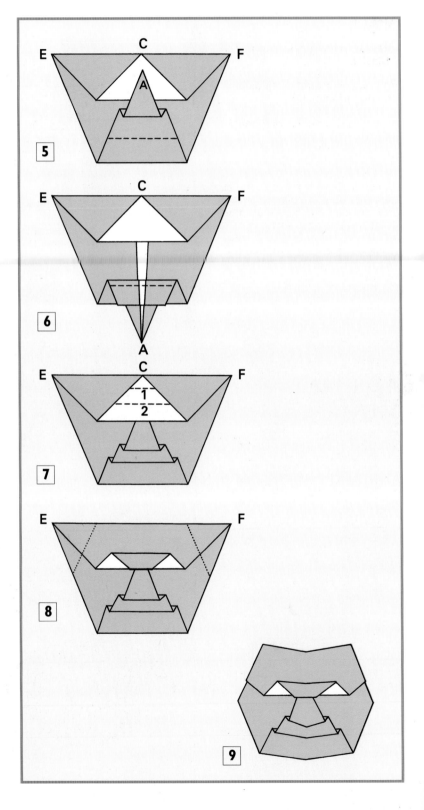